MW01643757

READ THIS SH*T WHEN YOU GET TIME

GEMINI JU

DEDICATION

This book is dedicated to the people crazy enough to bear their souls on paper and those who believe in the ability to silent the noises in their heads.

ACKNOWLEDGMENTS

I would like to express my deepest appreciation to my late mother, Cheryl Denise Robinson, the one person that taught me early in life that through artistic expression and creativity, I can conquer and control the voices of doubt within. I would also like to express my gratitude to those who helped inspire this body of work through hours of allowing me to ramble about the many voices that can plague the mind and from sharing meaningful dialogue about life with me.

DERELICTION OF DUTY

Our shameless failure to fulfill our duty to our brothers and sisters doesn't go unseen.
We so effortlessly step on each other's necks to obtain our selfish dream.
Whether it's for likes, views, or green.
We are quick to build ourselves up, while lowering the next person's self-esteem.
We have to do better with each other.
That was Malcom's, Martin's, Marcus' and the Minister's word.
We ignore that, abuse and misuse each other and refuse to ask for help, but our loud silence goes unheard.
The system abuses us, then we temporarily unite so that we may be seen and heard.
The next day, breaking news, another one of us shot down dead on the curb.
They see and hear our pain.
But until we become united and a true "we", the deaf ears will go unchanged.

REFLECTION

What emotion does this writing trigger within you?

Has there ever been a time in your life where you experienced the emotion of this writing? If so, how did you resolve it?

THE MIND OF A MAD MAN

The mad man doesn't know that his mind is corrupt.
Corrupt by the evils that society has placed in front of him to send him into a tirade.
A façade that he can't truly enjoy because its not God-given, its man-made.
Crafted to send that once "sane man" into a state of depression.
A depression that grows darker as the world continues to move.
Stuck in a state of being stagnant, he has no option but to lose.
His soul and mind are riddled with intrusive thoughts that pierce the very fabric of his creation.
Numb to the truths as though he's heavily medicated and under sedation.
The voices continue to scream loud and beg and plead for liberation.
He's now a prisoner in his own mind.
And beaten down by his own hand.
History shows that today's mentally liberated king, was once considered a mad man.

REFLECTION

What emotion does this writing trigger within you?

Has there ever been a time in your life where you experienced the emotion of this writing? If so, how did you resolve it?

THE WONDERING HEART

The wondering heart grows curious.
Not curious of that which it is without.
But curious of that which is within.
The heart doesn't know love.
The heart only knows life.
It knows nothing more than you allow it to.
Loving something or someone with all of your heart is expressive but not true.
It says, "Hey I love you with everything that allows me to be."
But it doesn't say, "Hey, I love you so much that I'm willing to give you all of me."
The heart pumps blood, it doesn't foster emotions.
The mind controls feelings and thoughts.
Loving with all your heart, is an expression to show your devotion.
I often wonder why people devote themselves to a person or a cause that's bigger than them.
Because when the love is gone, the light that once shined, now grows dim.
From your loved ones and causes over time will depart.
Keep your mind pure when it comes to matters of the wondering heart.

REFLECTION

What emotion does this writing trigger within you?

Has there ever been a time in your life where you experienced the emotion of this writing? If so, how did you resolve it?

THE MORNING BLISS DOESN'T LAST FOREVER

The morning marks the end to the night before, not a new day.
There are no days.
There are only cold nights and blissful mornings.
Mornings signify the new beginning of time.
A constant reminder that it's ok to reset.
To start again.
That courageous morning attitude should be without sin.
The pure bliss that you have a chance to begin again.
The suspense of the unknown should send you into rejoicing cheers.
While at the same time unveiling those hidden fears.
Let the bliss of the morning move you.
But don't let the vibrant thoughts of your life in the morning lose you.
For the pains of the night lingers into the bliss of the morning.

REFLECTION

What emotion does this writing trigger within you?

Has there ever been a time in your life where you experienced the emotion of this writing? If so, how did you resolve it?

LIFE

There is no roadmap or perfect study guide to life.
Life is just that, life.
There will be twists and turns.
Bruises and burns.
There will be nights that you can't sleep.
And nights that all you can do is mourn and weep.
Loved ones will come.
Loved ones will go.
Don't rush your process because just like everything else, it takes time to grow.
Water your seeds and fertilize your dirt.
And understand that experience is bestowed upon those that do the work.
So dry your tears and pack light.
To experience this unscripted movie called life.
Assume that everyone is an actor, merely playing a role.
Don't allow anyone or anything to corrupt your morals, principles and soul.
Life is going to occur without your permission.
Conquer all your goals, love hard, laugh loud and leave the physical realm not wishing.
Live life.

REFLECTION

What emotion does this writing trigger within you?

Has there ever been a time in your life where you experienced the emotion of this writing? If so, how did you resolve it?

HIGHER

Aim high.
Spread your wings and soar.
Your potential has an endless amount like never before.
Soar so high that you surpass the moon.
Remain steadfast as your time will come soon.
The limits set upon you by society act as shackles to keep you marginalized.
Make them believe you are who you say you are and stand in their lies.
Your name may not be known, but your character holds weight.
Etch your name in the history books, it is never too late.
Soar higher than you've ever soared before.
Realizing your potential and accomplishing your dreams should leave you wanting more.

REFLECTION

What emotion does this writing trigger within you?

Has there ever been a time in your life where you experienced the emotion of this writing? If so, how did you resolve it?

THE DARK SIDE OF THE LIGHT

They see the smiles.
But they don't see the pain.
They see the highs.
But they ignore the lows.
They want you at your best.
But desert you when you endure stress.
They love your wins.
But quick to judge your sins.
You can give them your heart.
But they don't accept its imperfections.
They want your mind.
But they can't handle your thoughts.
They constantly do you wrong.
But want you to do them right.
Let the world know your name, as you emerge from the
darkness within the light.

REFLECTION

What emotion does this writing trigger within you?

Has there ever been a time in your life where you experienced the emotion of this writing? If so, how did you resolve it?

MY SOUL ON PAPER

The soul embodies who I am.
As I sit in a state of solitude.
Minding my thoughts so that I don't be thought of as mean and cruel.
My soul is calm and peaceful always.
It's my mind and heart that separate themselves from my soul as they part ways.
To know my soul is not to know my heart.
My heart knows no mercy.
As all signs of empathy depart.
My soul was given to me by a supreme power.
A power that no man can manipulate.
Not with gold or riches, nothing can make my soul deviate.
I'm a caring person that often cares too much.
Feeling like I'm invincible because God's hands are on me and I can sense his saving touch.
Sometimes my words get jumbled as I speak aloud.
Yet my soul remains alone as I stand in the midst of a crowd.
No one knows the real me, only perceptions.
To know my soul is to know me and understand that I'm a master of deception.
This paper gives me freedom.
Freedom of expression and freedom of thought.
As the evils of the world are forever giving chase, Lord please don't let me get caught.

REFLECTION

What emotion does this writing trigger within you?

Has there ever been a time in your life where you experienced the emotion of this writing? If so, how did you resolve it?

AM I SAFE

I have several emotions.
Emotions that could cause commotions.
Not commotions in a sense of disturbance.
But in a sense of nervousness.
A sense of anxiety.
A sense of I'm afraid to open up and let my true self be heard.
A sense of I'm afraid to let me true self be seen.
I'm so damn afraid that someone will say that I come off as mean.
I'm a recluse in solitude.
Afraid to open up to you.
Afraid to smile.
But willing to yell out of anger.
Walking down the dark road of danger.
Roaming within myself and emotions alone.
Eyes empty like a castle with no king and no throne.
Afraid to be judged.
Afraid to be loved.
Afraid to be hugged.
So I reject acceptance and love repeatedly.
Afraid that you will use what I share with you against me.
So I hide.
I hide from you and I hide from myself.
Bottling everything up inside to the point where I jeopardize my health.
So afraid to be exposed so I hide and save face.
If I told you the complexities of who I am, will you keep me safe?

REFLECTION

What emotion does this writing trigger within you?

Has there ever been a time in your life where you experienced the emotion of this writing? If so, how did you resolve it?

MY CONFLICTED SOUL

My soul has always been conflicted.
Battling between good and evil.
If the good outweighs the bad, I wonder how much it truly weighs.
I've always had a knack for attracting trouble.
I'd go to church on Sunday, leave and get back to the life of trouble.
I wanted to do right, but it's so easy to do wrong.
Lying to myself that I won't be on this road to destruction for too long.
The vehicle to my demise is traveling at an alarming rate.
My soul continues to conflict and agree with evil, while I'm making God wait.
I am the true definition of what happens when love presents itself and is truly hate.
My conflicted soul as pure as it may be, I can't escape.

REFLECTION

What emotion does this writing trigger within you?

Has there ever been a time in your life where you experienced the emotion of this writing? If so, how did you resolve it?

SUCCESS

The very thought of success is bittersweet.
Your first mistake was thinking that it was yours to keep.
You define success as what you may.
Stressing yourself to find it every day.
The success finds those that truly want it.
If you want it taken away, brag about it and flaunt it.
See the masses are fooled about what success truly means.
It doesn't mean getting to the money, dinero or cream.
Its waking up every day knowing that you've accomplished your dreams.
Don't take it for granted and don't misuse it.
Because in the blink of an eye and while you're flexing, you can lose it.
The dream comes first and then comes the work.
You have to mentally plant the seeds of success and physically water the dirt.
The bigger the dream the bigger the reward.
Battling the image in the mirror and self-doubt like a knight swinging his sword.
The camera, the snaps, the glitz and the glam.
The success of money is always curtailed by your good ole Uncle Sam.
They tax your life.
They tax your dream.
On the road to success try not to lose steam.
Your dream, your hustle, your smile, your strife.
Find peace in knowing that the first step to success is accepting your life.

REFLECTION

What emotion does this writing trigger within you?

Has there ever been a time in your life where you experienced the emotion of this writing? If so, how did you resolve it?

EVERYTHING HAS A PRICE

Everything has a price.
Your integrity.
Your morals.
Your principles.
Your life.
Don't ever say "my soul isn't for sale."
Knowing damn well you sold it to the devil years ago and you didn't know it had a price because you didn't ask for a single detail.
Now you're feeling derailed.
Out of touch with yourself.
Fret not though because over the years you've acquired a lot of wealth.
Jeopardizing your health.
Now your integrity and health are compromised because the devil wrote you that check himself.
He didn't send his collectors to collect your soul.
He just showed you the highway and reminded you to be ready to make that payment at the toll.
You better be ready to say "present" when he calls that roll.
Your spirit, mind and principles make up your soul.
Don't ever be put in a position like you're at an auction and they put a sign on your back that says sold.
You went to the highest bidder and now you're infectious just like black mold.
How much did you sell your morals for?
Was it a dollar and a quarter or much more?
You went to the highest soul corrupter like a biblical whore.
And your existence is no more.
Don't be surprised when no one answers heaven's door.
Now you're wandering because you're lost.
Because you sold your life at a cheap cost.
Now you answer to a soul boss.
Not a boss like a 9 to 5.
But a boss that controls your will to survive.
Now your cost drops day to day.

And you don't know what to say.
You physically arrive at 6 and your soul handlers arrived at 8.
I ask you again, how much did it take?
You abuse your own people to just barely stay ahead.
Not realizing that although you're the life of the party, your soul been dead.
You feared that who you are and what you had wouldn't suffice.
So one last time I ask you, what was your price?

REFLECTION

What emotion does this writing trigger within you?

Has there ever been a time in your life where you experienced the emotion of this writing? If so, how did you resolve it?

PROTECT YOUR PEACE

Protect your peace.
Rid your life of things and people that jeopardize it.
If they don't add to your life then they should at least stabilize it.
Empathize with it.
Most people don't care, so they can't sympathize with it.
People will literally drain you.
Blame you.
And then shame you.
Then leave you traumatized with it.
Don't allow their energies and insults patronize and demonize it.
Then when you're unbothered they will act out, put on a show, you know dramatize it.
Instead of being God's child and humanize it.
Or if you act out and get mad then they villainize it.
Your peace is costly, so you better prioritize it.
Normalize it.
Your peace ain't for everyone so don't democratize it.
Take your peace and immortalize it.
Organize it.
No matter how much it gets tested,
Don't ever cut ties with it.
Protect yours.

REFLECTION

What emotion does this writing trigger within you?

Has there ever been a time in your life where you experienced the emotion of this writing? If so, how did you resolve it?

THE LAW OF SUPPLY AND DEMAND

We are the supply.
And the demand is high.
It's not a demand for our intelligence and meaningful things we can provide.
It's a demand for the prison system to take a black body and hide.
They got a demand.
And we got the supply.
As soon as you are born, they assign you a number so that you're easy to identify.
See we know right from wrong and endure the struggle at home.
Yet we still supply them with bodies to fill those beds in that barbwire and heavily guarded home.
They don't care about your character if that quota is met.
In the blink of an eye you're waiting to get stripped searched as the guard yells next.
Your basic rights are taken.
Your freedom is revoked.
All you got left is a wish and fading hope.
Wishing they'd give you another chance.
Hoping that you make parole.
You've paid your debt, but you still get denied because they have yet to reach their goal.
See the goal is numbers, not crime control.
Free labor to their investors as they count their gold.
The wealthy gets wealthier.
And the poor goes to prison.
The system isn't broken, it is working in lines with their vision.
Stripped us of our rich heritage and made prisons our lingering tradition.
The demand wont end.
But the supply must grow thin.
Lady justice peeking through that blind fold is another one of America's sins.
Justice isn't blind.

They will claim it every time.
Especially because America denies its biggest sin.
You being a good supply for their demand, shouldn't be
determined by the color of your skin.

REFLECTION

What emotion does this writing trigger within you?

Has there ever been a time in your life where you experienced the emotion of this writing? If so, how did you resolve it?

I'M YOUR ANCESTORS' WORST NIGHTMARE

I'm your ancestors' worst nightmare.
From my ability to articulate my words and tame my hair.
They prolly pissed turning in their grave.
Mad because they never envisioned a sambo having it this made.
I can vote.
I can read.
I can write.
This ain't a nonviolent movement these days, I like to fight.
I fight with my words and use my mind.
Even though they are passing racist laws, this ain't the Jim Crow Era, ain't no traveling back in time.
I look forward to the promise to remember from whence we came.
If I don't obtain this so-called "American Dream", I'm the one to blame.
See my ancestors died for me.
Your ancestors died trying to stop progress.
My ancestors locked in and endured bearings, and they never trusted the process.
From strange fruit.
To planting the seeds and growing roots.
My ancestors stood strong, kind of like a New Yorker in some timberland boots.
I'm your ancestors' worst nightmare.
I know you probably can't believe it.
My ancestors foreshadowed my success even when I couldn't foresee it.
They knew a change was coming.
All the time while running.
To, not from the Bull Conners and his wild dogs, all while humming.
Hymns of prosperity.
Singing songs of disparity.
Hoping that God saves them all and provide clarity.

Clarity of this New America.
Hoping that it will be better for my generation and your generation.
Praying that we didn't have to deal with the evils of segregation.
See my ancestors had a vision that together, America could make it.
Praying that your ancestors understand their pain and could see the effects of their own hatred.
But how can a blind man see the color of his own eyes?
How can a compulsive liar start to believe his own lies.
I know right now my ancestors are laughing and joking like "my my, how time flies."
No more yessuh massa.
No more driving Ms. Daisy.
America was built on the backs of my ancestors but today you call us lazy.
That nonsense is shady.
America's political system is crazy.
Who could have ever imagined that for looking at a white woman you could be penalized.
This day and age, we are energized.
Your perception of me was inherited from your ancestors, so you're compromised.
I'm your ancestors' worst nightmare because I'm my ancestors' potential realized.

REFLECTION

What emotion does this writing trigger within you?

Has there ever been a time in your life where you experienced the emotion of this writing? If so, how did you resolve it?

HUMANITY

The definition of humanity is really the entire human race.
So often time its definition and true meaning is misplaced.
From the seas at the end of the Earth.
To the skies that were first given birth.
There is only one race.
And it's the human race.
There is no black.
There is no white.
There is only what's good or bad.
And what's wrong or right.
The wicked and soulless will continue to control the night.
The barbarians were separated from the civilized.
And then the civilized were villainized.
The blessed became the cursed.
And the barbarians became the well versed.
Versed in the evils.
Versed in the peril.
Versed in leaving a blessed people sterile.
The humanity in the human race is about love and helping others.
God never intended to create enemies and have people hurt one another.
We have to do better.

REFLECTION

What emotion does this writing trigger within you?

Has there ever been a time in your life where you experienced the emotion of this writing? If so, how did you resolve it?

THE MASK

The mask that we wear conceals the soul.
It hides our inner being in warmth and cold.
This mask doesn't allow for the true you to be alive.
It prevents your soul from being able to thrive.
Growth requires light, confidence, and nourishment.
Growth doesn't take into account an empty compliment.
The mask casts shadows on the inner workings of who you are.
Who you strive to be.
The mask you wear and live in isn't free.
It comes with a price.
The price is unfathomable, especially when the cost is leading
an unfulfilling life.

REFLECTION

What emotion does this writing trigger within you?

Has there ever been a time in your life where you experienced the emotion of this writing? If so, how did you resolve it?

IS THE SKY TRULY THE LIMIT?

If the sky is endless how can it be the limit?
If your stars align with the universe then they are all complicit.
Complicit in your elevation.
Conspiring with your personal dedication.
Preparing you for your transformation.
And giving you your much needed liberation.
Or is the so-called limit just a figment of the imagination?
Created to keep you in line.
Created without your true potential in mind.
Does the sky end where the universe begin?
If not, then your potential for greatness has no end.

REFLECTION

What emotion does this writing trigger within you?

Has there ever been a time in your life where you experienced the emotion of this writing? If so, how did you resolve it?

PAIN'S GRACE

Love is erratic.
Pain is calming.
Attempting to find the balance between the two can sometimes be alarming.
Often misused.
Most times, confused.
The two concepts are interchangeable and overly abused.
Pain comes with love.
Love comes with pain.
Throughout life, both are impossible to completely maintain.
The broken dreams.
Followed by a warm cunning embrace.
Comes blurring memories that you can't retrace.
Loving through the pain, gives pain the sweetest grace.

REFLECTION

What emotion does this writing trigger within you?

Has there ever been a time in your life where you experienced the emotion of this writing? If so, how did you resolve it?

THE EPIDEMIC

The epidemic is everlasting.
Not the literal use of drugs, VCRs being pawned or families clashing.
I'm talking about the strongest drug known to mankind.
The type of drug that will make the true you hard to find.
Hard to find because you're not the same.
The drug is called fame.
Fame is a lil scary sumn.
That shit will have you on sucka media frontin.
Frontin on others, frontin on the trolls and frontin on yourself.
Posing by other people cars knowing damn well you haven't acquired any type of wealth.
Why you think you only standing by the Maybach and not sitting in it.
Secured like three brands deals and got merch instead of bread because they knew you didn't know how to spend it.
See you try to align yourself with the haves.
Praying that they break off more than a little of half.
Thinking that people really support you when you're really the joke that trigger the laughs.
Stretching yourself thin, up and down getting stretched out like calisthenics on your calves.
Bitter and cavalier like when that star leaves you and now you wanna watch them burn like the cavs.
Your soul is depleted.
Because your favorite celebrity that you keep @'n, they won't retweet it.
Mad at the winners because you feel defeated.
Obsoleted.
Not needed.
Now you walking funny for likes on the gram you knew, knock-kneeded.
Dying on the inside and screaming for attention.
Smiling from ear to ear as soon as you get the notification that you're got a mention.
It's a dm from God telling you that your soul is missing.

REFLECTION

What emotion does this writing trigger within you?

Has there ever been a time in your life where you experienced the emotion of this writing? If so, how did you resolve it?

SUFFOCATING AIR

The air is thick and full of resentment.
The deep breaths I take create my lack of contentment.
The air is full of hate.
I slow down my breathing to preserve my fate.
The energy radiating from those around me is off.
I'm trying not to breathe the same air they breathe so that I don't get lost.
Lost in the crowd and assume an identity that's not mine.
Their intentions are clear and their motives are defined.
The air is heavy and full of judgment.
Their eyes are on me trying to figure out my temperament.
My lungs are filled with evil that I breathed in.
Why am I being responsible and taking on their character, this was their sin.
Their sin to own.
Mine to disown.
I refuse to lose myself to a crowd where who they are to themselves is unknown.
Their energy emits like they're defecating.
The air that people let out and you take in can be suffocating.

REFLECTION

What emotion does this writing trigger within you?

Has there ever been a time in your life where you experienced the emotion of this writing? If so, how did you resolve it?

THE DARKEST HOURS BLOOMS THE MOST BEAUTIFUL FLOWER

In the pitch-black hours of the night.
In your darkest moments during your internal fight.
In the depths of your soul there is a forever shinning light.
The struggle that you endure on a daily basis doesn't go unnoticed.
But that fight builds character and helps bloom your beautiful lotus.
Rise from the ashes.
Rise from the dirt.
Your blossoming season is here, your new petals signify your rebirth.
Plant your roots when no one is watching.
Nurture your soul so that your appearance is shocking.
Allow your pure blossoms time to grow.
Emerge yourself in the depths of the darkness as they are not shallow.
So when you emerge don't allow your radiance to cower.
Allow your darkest moments to bloom you into your most beautiful flower.

REFLECTION

What emotion does this writing trigger within you?

Has there ever been a time in your life where you experienced the emotion of this writing? If so, how did you resolve it?

I DON'T LOOK LIKE WHAT I'VE BEEN THROUGH

I never accept defeat.
I will never know how to retreat.
I will never allow myself to stay down long.
My mind and my drive are entirely too strong.
To accept defeat is to kill your goal.
Take a stand, stand firm, and grab a hold.
Grit your teeth and plant your feet.
For your appearance alone will not allow you to accept defeat.
The war against you rages on.
Stand up for what you believe in even if you stand alone.
A bloody brow and a scar ridden body.
Fight so damn hard to get back to you that the memories of almost defeated are foggy.
The internal scars can never be erased.
Use them as fuel to help you finish your race.
Don't ever allow the self-doubting enemy win and defeat you.
You're intact still because you don't look like what you've been through.
You may feel defeated.
And you may wish you would have retreated.
Finish your race and finish the fight so that you don't feel cheated.
Cheated from a chance to test your limits.
Missing the opportunity to know that you did it.
You defeated defeat.
You made retreating retreat.
You didn't allow yourself to remain in that heap.
The heap of pain.
The heap of sorrow.
Fight through today for there is an amazing tomorrow.
When they ask what's troubling you.
Swiftly remind them that you do not look like what you've been through.

REFLECTION

What emotion does this writing trigger within you?

Has there ever been a time in your life where you experienced the emotion of this writing? If so, how did you resolve it?

PHAROAH'S DILEMMA

Don't ever cut your nose to spite your face.
Don't be so fast to move,
Keep a steady pace.
Don't be so ego-driven that you drive others away.
Don't be so complacent that you can't make a way.
Don't become nose-less by being cynical.
Wisdom is within you, as you are a king, it's biblical.
Accept what is and accept what can never be.
Don't allow others to make you nose-less and alter your imagery.
You are a king bearing God's blood and presence.
Don't let their perception of you destroy your God-given King essence.
Don't let society dictate the size of your nose.
Be committed to owning your truth that you were chose.
Chosen to be the natural people.
Chosen to lead the people from evil.
Through the riches and the fame.
Keep your nose the same.
Don't overreact to needless things.
Avoid the pharaoh's dilemma and embrace the change.
Soften your temper.
But don't bow your bloodied head.
Don't be a pushover, be resolute and mild mannered to the evils amongst you instead.

REFLECTION

What emotion does this writing trigger within you?

Has there ever been a time in your life where you experienced the emotion of this writing? If so, how did you resolve it?

I'M AN OVER-THINKER

I'm in my head.
More than you in your bed.
And you lazy.
I'm sure when people hear me talking to myself, they be like yeah he crazy.
I'm not delusional though.
I'm really just trying to decide which direction I want to go.
The good or the bad.
The happy or the sad.
I really can't control the process.
Me talking to all my personalities is just a part of my decision-making process.
The whispers grow heavy.
The conversation is steady.
Everyone has a valid point.
The calmer me wins as I hit this pre-rolled joint.
The voices are silenced.
The creativity is flowing.
All the while my insecurities and overthinking is steadily growing.
I try to escape it.
I try to ignore it.
So I embrace it.
So that I don't destroy it.
The voices are at war.
The mindfulness of me that have, I adore.
I'm in my head.
I'm an over-thinker.
And an over-stander.
I over-stand the complexities of life and I keep my words short so that there is no slander.
I need a way out.
What's their end game?
Are they using me?
If so, then that shit lame.

But it's impossible to use me because I already figured them out.
They continue to pay me compliments.
I wonder what's that about?
They come off as being genuine.
But the compliments sound like a snake hiss.
Surely if I plan my escape properly, there's no way things can go amiss.
I'm in my head.
They can tell that I don't trust.
I have to get out of my head before I self-destruct, it's a must.

REFLECTION

What emotion does this writing trigger within you?

Has there ever been a time in your life where you experienced the emotion of this writing? If so, how did you resolve it?

THE EYES TELL THE POET'S TELL

The eyes of the poet tells the story.
The story of where a person has been. His pain, his glory.
The depth of the eyes bears the truth.
From celebratory praises of the first black president back to the pickings of strange fruit.
The eyes bear the gateway to the soul and to your truth.
It can't conceal the pain and horrors of life that you've been through.
From the dark and piercing stares.
To the brightness like flares.
The eyes will forever bear the poet's tell.
Tell your story how you will, subject to your own demise.
But for the truth, tell your story through your poetic eyes.

REFLECTION

What emotion does this writing trigger within you?

Has there ever been a time in your life where you experienced the emotion of this writing? If so, how did you resolve it?

YOUR LIFE, YOUR CREATION

Create the life that you envision.
Your dream is your vision.
The life you want starts as a blank sheet.
Use the brightest of colors to paint the life that you foresee.
Be the artist.
Be the composer.
Develop your film in the dark room so that the imagery gets the right amount of exposure.
Be creative and be defiant.
Your life, your creation, is self-reliant.
The type of image you create depends upon you.
Use your resources and choose your hue.
Don't attempt to be exact.
Remain adaptable and be abstract.
So that the mysteries and unknowns of life and your creation are intact.
Follow your own rubric and continue to compose.
Accept your final masterpiece as indicative of the life you chose.

REFLECTION

What emotion does this writing trigger within you?

Has there ever been a time in your life where you experienced the emotion of this writing? If so, how did you resolve it?

FOES DISGUISED AS FRIENDS

The masks that foes and friends wear look familiar.
Then they start to look similar.
But when you get a glance of them under the light of true colors, they start to look peculiar.
Their lies line up perpendicular.
Then they run over your pride and try to kill your dreams like a homicide that's vehicular.
The hate in their eyes resemble admiration.
They try to pass degradation as constructive elevation.
It's an abomination.
That requires classification.
And identification.
Of who truly has your best interest at heart.
And who is possibly just playing the part.
It's a mystery that needs solving.
Friend or foe, foe or friend, the two are forever moving like a door that's revolving.
Who can you trust?
Or is being able to trust a must?
It's a scary situation.
Especially when you have foes who are friends and friends who are foes and you make a misidentification.

REFLECTION

What emotion does this writing trigger within you?

Has there ever been a time in your life where you experienced the emotion of this writing? If so, how did you resolve it?

A SINNER'S BIGGEST SIN

A sinner's biggest sin is being judgmental.
We judge those that sin like us as if the judgmental is just coincidental.
Coincidental to the sinner.
Coincidental to the sin.
On a scale of one to ten.
There is nothing more hypocritical than a sinner judging another's sin.
They say judge not, lest ye be judged.
Your sin record isn't clean, in fact it's severely smudged.
Your high horse is lower than it was before.
Your sins don't wash away as shells do when high tide comes ashore.
Be not the judge of another's action.
As outcasting the sinner will not bring you satisfaction.
A sin is a sin no matter the gravity.
Your sin is your sin as it is your reality.
Plague not your mind as it could decide your mortality.
Immoral or not, don't criticize another's morality.
The judges will be judged for their iniquities.
Before you sit in judgment of others, be sure you are without deficiencies.

REFLECTION

What emotion does this writing trigger within you?

Has there ever been a time in your life where you experienced the emotion of this writing? If so, how did you resolve it?

THE ROSE IS REALLY A CACTUS

You're really a cactus, posing as a rose.
Both have thorns but one is twice as cold.
See the cactus is ugly to the eye and prickly indeed.
But on the inside, it has sustenance that can give you what you need.
It can quench your thirst with just a sip.
While that rose is appealing but gives a lot of lip.
The rose commands attention and is easily hurt.
While that cactus stands tall and silent surrounded naturally by dirt.
See the dirt and cactus represent by any means you will grow.
While that rose needs too much maintenance and attention before it can even grow.
As it has many imperfections and doesn't look as appealing as the rose, no matter what, that cactus will grow.

REFLECTION

What emotion does this writing trigger within you?

Has there ever been a time in your life where you experienced the emotion of this writing? If so, how did you resolve it?

MATRIX

The matrix.
A fabrication of ideas that aren't reality.
From the clothes you wear to the righteous than thou personality.
Nothing is real.
But yet nothing is fake.
Brands use the haves to plant their stake.
Society uses the haves to sell an idea.
Leaving the have nots in conditions that aren't ideal.
The red or the blue pill.
Which one represents the truth?
So busy chasing a fantasy that you forgo your youth.
Lost in a land where silence is a loud scream.
Haunted by nightmares called the American Dream.
Scorned by the desires of the want to acquire wealth.
Ignorant as to why intellectuals operate in stealth.
If all the world's a stage as suggested by Shakespeare.
That would explain why the players on the stage continue to adhere.
Adhere to the masses.
Adhere to the brands.
Afraid to break free from illusory shackles that bound their hands.
Don't be a slave to those imaginary things.
The matrix can be broken easily simply by cutting your stings.
The strings from fabrications that keep you attached.
Don't place emphasis on material things and become detached.
The truth is what you perceive it to be.

REFLECTION

What emotion does this writing trigger within you?

Has there ever been a time in your life where you experienced the emotion of this writing? If so, how did you resolve it?

THE EFFECT

You are the butterfly effect.
Small but impactful and very direct.
Your presence is unknown but yet it demands respect.
A small sequence of events and you can change the course of history.
No one truly knows the impact that you can have so it remains a mystery.
A mystery to them but destiny to you.
Spread your wings.
Alter the landscape.
And see it through.
Things can change by you taking a leap of faith.
Be mindful of your actions as they can be scathe.
Beautiful and peaceful but yet so powerful.
You're a necessary to the future as your gifts are desirable.
As quickly as you act your impact will be swift.
When you strike, strike hard, disrupt things and cause a rift.

REFLECTION

What emotion does this writing trigger within you?

Has there ever been a time in your life where you experienced the emotion of this writing? If so, how did you resolve it?

NOBODY CARES, DO THE WORK

Yesterday's win was yesterday's win focus on the next.
Accept, smile, strategize and reflect.
There is no time for cheers and pointless applause.
There is no destination in your future when you move without cause.
No congratulatory celebrations are everlasting.
The ooohs and ahhs and we are proud of you aren't long-lasting.
The lights can be contagious with admiration in their stares.
Stop trying to appease others and just do the work because nobody cares.
A long day will be followed by a victorious night.
Even without their claps and confetti you should always stand upright.
Through grins and laughter and even a smirk.
Remember that nobody cares, so you have to do the work.
Work hard so that you yourself are very proud.
And your cheers of self-accomplishment will ring loud amongst the crowd.
Reliance on others can leave you scarred.
In being legendary, the want is easy but the work is hard.
Standing alone and losing battles will have their despairs.
But remember to stand firm, stand tall and be bold because nobody cares.

REFLECTION

What emotion does this writing trigger within you?

Has there ever been a time in your life where you experienced the emotion of this writing? If so, how did you resolve it?

BE LEGENDARY

Legends never die.
As they leave the physical realm, they live in the sky.
Not in a spiritual sense like heaven and hell.
But one where their existence is that of a fairytale.
They did the work and endured the pain.
And when they're gone, they've made a name.
They perspired blood and took the criticism.
As onlookers look and judge with skepticism.
They're called defiant and even cynical.
Often deemed to be as*holes and egotistical.
But it's the drive and will to be great that makes them legends.
The fear of being average leaves them threatened.
They adopt habits and a work ethic that are second to none.
Chasing ghosts and constantly improving is their type of fun.
So bear witness to the blinded visionary.
As they chase immortality and become legendary.
Be Legendary.

REFLECTION

What emotion does this writing trigger within you?

Has there ever been a time in your life where you experienced the emotion of this writing? If so, how did you resolve it?

THE DEAD END

The dead end is just that, a dead end.
The road ends.
And the smiles end where the frown begins.
Numbing days in a pointless place.
Drains the life and youth out of your face.
The energy that you exude is overly contagious.
Existing in a lifeless situation is disadvantageous.
Rid yourself of the dead end day.
As complacency is not a justification to stay.
Your true purpose is that for which you exist.
You avoid the battle with your destiny as though you are a pacifist.
Endure the fight and prepare for the war.
The manner in which you accept defeat is abhor.
Stand against the sun rising and setting on your potential.
Because your gifts to the world are what make you essential.
Unbury your gifts and pave the way.
As the road that was once a dead end, will change into a one-way.
Follow your dreams and utilize your gifts.

REFLECTION

What emotion does this writing trigger within you?

Has there ever been a time in your life where you experienced the emotion of this writing? If so, how did you resolve it?

THE PROFESSIONAL VICTIM

The professional victim.
Always looking for a villain.
Tormenting those around them because they truly need healing.
Shrewd to the core and always picking fights.
Bullying those around them who aren't willing to tell them they're right.
Ignoring advice and negating common sense.
Always finding a way to make every interaction with them intense.
Fighting a fighter-less battle with ghostlike opponents.
Sucking the life out of the party and the joy out of moments.
They present themselves as strong and are often weak mentally.
Always comparing themselves to others and acting jealously.
Nobody likes me.
Nobody understands.
Not willing to accept who they are which the truth demands.
You're a professional victim.
Cowering in hate.
You're a professional victim.
Always ready to berate.
You're a professional victim.
But never the aggressor.
You're a professional victim.
Always the oppressed but never the oppressor.

REFLECTION

What emotion does this writing trigger within you?

Has there ever been a time in your life where you experienced the emotion of this writing? If so, how did you resolve it?

WHAT DO I OWE?

Do I owe you for giving me your time?
Or do I owe you for me giving you mine?
What do I owe you from being in your presence?
Or is it illusory's essence?
I hope your friendship doesn't come with a cost?
I'm asking because in most cases the truth is lost.
Lost due to falsehoods and forced laughs.
The valuable lessons learned in our lives crossing paths.
If it comes with suppressing the true you.
If it costs, then let me know what's due?
If it costs more than being who I am.
Or does the genuineness resemble a scam?

REFLECTION

What emotion does this writing trigger within you?

Has there ever been a time in your life where you experienced the emotion of this writing? If so, how did you resolve it?

THE ETERNAL WAR

Life is an enteral war.
No winners.
No losers.
Just soldiers.
Soldiers who will all meet the same fate.
An end to their existence.
A chance to meet their makers.
Giving in a life to a world full do takers.
But all the while, the war goes on.
No more dusk no more dawn.
Just darkness.
Cold darkness.
The battle will continue on.
No praises, no boos, it's all gone.
Life is a continuing cycle of imaginary victories and defeats.
Knowing this, why allow your strategy to succeed in life decrease?
So fight the winner-less and defeat-less fight.
Live for glory now because your past you can't rewrite.
The eternal war is forevermore.
Just as it begins and never ends, the war is a revolving door.

REFLECTION

What emotion does this writing trigger within you?

Has there ever been a time in your life where you experienced the emotion of this writing? If so, how did you resolve it?

GENUINELY INAUTHENTIC

I sometimes wonder if they even realize that they are fake.
Maybe they've pretended so long that they don't even realize that they move as a snake.
Maybe they're ignorant as to what it means to be a decent person.
They will betray you a million times and not even realize that who they are is uncertain.
You feel the pain of their actions.
But you're split on what to do like its fractions.
You're left to be only a portion of who you truly are.
But they don't care because they don't take the deceit and live with it.
Maybe they don't even know that they're genuinely inauthentic.

REFLECTION

What emotion does this writing trigger within you?

Has there ever been a time in your life where you experienced the emotion of this writing? If so, how did you resolve it?

CRACK-LIKE HABITS

A habit that's detrimental to your wellbeing is like crack.
It's easy to get.
It's easy to hit.
But it's leaves a weird smell that sticks.
A bad habit can cost you your teeth and your health.
Just like a crack habit can rob you of your wealth.
The habits you keep can increase or decrease the company you keep.
Meanwhile your soul is still deteriorating from where you and bad habits meet.
A pathway to the dead end that looked like an intersection.
Thinking you had options when your destiny off that high aroma was always headed in the wrong direction.
Lost and confused
While others sit back and are amused.
By your constant struggles.
Your constant pain.
But you are too high to notice because you're watching yourself roam this earth lost through your soul's windowpane.
As the lighter flame grows.

REFLECTION

What emotion does this writing trigger within you?

Has there ever been a time in your life where you experienced the emotion of this writing? If so, how did you resolve it?

I LOVE ME

I choose me to love.
I choose me to rise above.
Above the self-conscious perceptions of me.
As I look in the mirror I study me carefully.
A dark wide nose.
With a bright angelic soul.
These are my inner thoughts that can no longer go untold.
I admire my own resolve.
I love the fact that in any circumstances, I know how to evolve.
Evolve into who it is I need to be.
Nah this ain't being two-faced but you may see it differently.
See I love me so much that I'm multiple people all in one.
I'm friendly one day and the next we done.
I love the fact that I'm a complicated soul.
That is willing to not leave those inner thoughts untold.
I love me so much that it may seem like I hate you.
I don't hate you.
I just finally chose me over you.
I love me so much that I'm willing to own my flaws.
I love me so much that I can ignore the criticisms of all.
Self-love is the best.
Self-assessment can be a mess.
Accepting you for you can be a daunting task.
Look in the mirror, accept who you are and remove that mask.
I love me.

REFLECTION

What emotion does this writing trigger within you?

Has there ever been a time in your life where you experienced the emotion of this writing? If so, how did you resolve it?

I FALL SHORT

I often fall short of who I aspire to be.
Having demonic like experiences while I'm watching me.
As the day breaks, I view myself as a part of the fakes.
For not holding true to who I say I am.
Reminding myself that this is real life, no filter, not glitz, no gram.
I built a life that I've always wanted.
Never posting it on social media because I know others want it.
But what do I do?
Risk it all for selfish pleasures and manipulative desires.
Feeling my soul withering away as my time here expires.
I fall short of who I prayed to be.
Knowing all along that my biggest op is me.
Operating with a selfish mindset.
Rolling loaded dice praying for a fair bet.
Looking in the mirror and not recognizing the soul that looks back.
Normally a radiant person but now my soul feels black.
Not black as in dark but black as in lost.
Bank account looking pretty good but I still can't afford the cost.
The cost of suffrage.
No monies to cover it.

REFLECTION

What emotion does this writing trigger within you?

Has there ever been a time in your life where you experienced the emotion of this writing? If so, how did you resolve it?

PAIN

The trauma is undeniable.
It can alter the very thoughts that your life is on track.
You're lost moving forward but refusing to look back.
The trauma that's endured often goes unspoken.
The family keeps the secrets to appear as though it is unbroken.
From mental, sexual and physical abuse.
The silence doesn't erase it, the silence is a noose.
The pain created.
Leaves true feeling evaded.
The sick thoughts creep into the pain filled mind.
Visibly shaken to the core, but yet they act blind.
Blind to the blurred vision of deception.
Viewing your coping as acceptance.
You feel hopeless.
Often blaming yourself for another's mistake.
So much pain.
With very little to gain.
They don't understand because they ignore your detrimental behavior.
All the while you just wanted a savior.
Someone to save you from your pain.
Someone to save you from yourself.
Someone to save you from the evils that plague your brain.
As you deal with the everlasting, unbearable pain.

REFLECTION

What emotion does this writing trigger within you?

Has there ever been a time in your life where you experienced the emotion of this writing? If so, how did you resolve it?

I'M GOOD

I'm good even when I'm really not.
When asked am I sure, I reply that's all I got.
I'm good because even when I'm not, I am.
I don't have the luxury to cover my wounds with filters from the gram.
My soul cries loud but silent.
My mouth says I'm good but my eyes are defiant.
Defiant and in conflict with the truth.
The truth that I only say I'm good to appease you.
Appease you so that you don't have to worry.
Or try to carry my burden.
The burden of fear.
The burden of self-hate.
The burden of determining which path in life I wish to take.
The burden of being a king in this unknown land without a crown.
The burden of not earning enough and letting you down.
The burden of shame and hiding behind lies.
The burden of seeing disappointment in my kids' eyes.
The burdens run heavy and the pain runs deep.
My eyes remain dry and ice cold but inside I weep.
Not feeling the need or want to explain what will be misunderstood.
So anytime you ask me how I am.
My response will always be "I'm good".

REFLECTION

What emotion does this writing trigger within you?

Has there ever been a time in your life where you experienced the emotion of this writing? If so, how did you resolve it?

GET YOU A THERAPIST AND GET THAT SH*T OUT.
DON'T ALLOW YOUR HEALING PROCESS TO ESCAPE YOU.
BREAK THE STEREOTYPE AND HEAL.

Made in the USA
Columbia, SC
23 July 2025

0c72bba4-93ea-4d06-8dc7-ba086fa5d29cR01